HOW TO FIX ALMOST ANYTHING

First published in 2007 by Five Areas.
This edition first published in 2012 by Darton, Longman and Todd Ltd
1 Spencer Court, 140–142 Wandsworth High Street, London SW18 4JJ.

Copyright © 2007 Dr Chris Williams. The right of Dr Chris Williams to be identified as the compiler of this work has been asserted in accordance with the Copyright, Designs and Patents Act 1998.

ISBN 978-0-232-52916-6

A catalogue record for this book is available from the British Library.
Printed and bound in Great Britain by Halstan & Co Ltd, Amersham.

Although we hope you find this book helpful, it's not intended to be a direct substitute for consultative advice with a healthcare professional, nor does the author or the publisher give any assurances about its effectiveness in a particular case. Accordingly, neither the author nor the publisher shall be held liable for any loss or damages arising from its use.

HOW TO FIX ALMOST ANYTHING

IN FOUR EASY STEPS

Dr Chris Williams

DARTON·LONGMAN+TODD

Finish a Project
Lose some weight
GET A JOB
STOP OVERSPENDING
Get Fitter
REVISE FOR EXAMS
DRINK LESS
Make more friends
Get out more
PLAN FOR A HOLIDAY

Yes, almost everything

It doesn't matter what you want to do, this easy 4-step plan will help you do it.

It works particularly well if you're feeling low. In fact it works even if you're so fed up you can only just be bothered reading this page.

The idea is to break your problem or target into tiny little chunks that, by themselves, are easy to do.

Then you work out how you're going to do each chunk, make a plan, and carry it out. It's called the Easy 4-Step Plan (E4SP for short).

It's like eating an elephant.

E4SP STEP 1

HOW TO EAT AN ELEPHANT

a. Break elephant into small chunks
b. Eat one chunk at a time

Problems are like elephants

They look huge. Far too big to deal with. But when you break them into bits, they're much less frightening and a lot easier to fix (or eat). That's why step 1 of the E4SP is 'break your problem into pieces'.

Let's say you you feel you never get out. You could break the week into bits and decide to do something on Mondays, for example.If you want to get out more, don't try and become a party animal yet – just work on a little bit of the problem – like leaving the house or walking round the park.

Or if you're spending too much, you could start by just cutting out online shopping. Most tasks can be chopped up like this, and everyone* agrees that you're much more likely to succeed when you do things bit by bit.

*Everyone except elephants.

Turn over for **STEP 2**

E4SP STEP 2

BRAINSTORM WAYS TO DO THE FIRST PIECE

Grab a piece of paper...

And write down all the things you could do to work on the first bit of the problem.

The trick with brainstorming is to let your mind run free, and write everything down – the whacky things as well as the sensible ones.

To get out more on Mondays, for example, you could join an evening class or go to the pictures on Mondays (so you don't just sit in at home).

If you're working on getting out of the house, you might buy a book on trees and try and spot four new types every day as you walk home through the park.

Trying to cut down online shopping? Use the parental controls in your browser to lock yourself out of the sites you spend money on.

If you write everything down, there's bound to be a good idea in there somewhere.

STEP 3 next

E4SP STEP 3

CHOOSE AN IDEA AND MAKE A PLAN TO DO IT

Step by step

Look at your brainstorm ideas and pick one. Choose one that looks do-able and doesn't scare you too much. Now take another piece of paper and write down, step by step, how to actually DO it. Make the steps as small as you like: Get up. Get dressed. Walk to front door. Open door ... and so on.

OR

To get out more on Mondays: Go to evening class tomorrow. Go in and ask about courses. Sign up for Monday night's class ... like that.

OR

For online shopping: Open Explorer. Go to Tools. Go to security settings. Add shopping sites to the restricted zone (or whatever variation of this you need to do on your particular browser) ...

Make sure that the steps are small, straightforward and seem like things you could really do.

What if something gets in the way?

As soon as you've written your plan, think about what could stop it happening. Are there any things that might trip you up? What about other people? Could someone be unhelpful at any stage?

When you've figured out what might block your progress, work out another mini-plan for getting round the obstacle.

This way, you'll be ready for whatever happens!

Final step coming up

E4SP STEP 4

CHECK THE PLAN AND PUT IT INTO ACTION

This is it! You've written down all the steps, now you need to check that they're do-able. Use this checklist:

Is it realistic?
You're not planning to run a marathon are you?

Are you aiming at just one thing?
Don't try and do more than one item on your list. You can always pick another when you've sorted the first one.

Is it slow?
There's no need to rush at things. Your plan can take as long as you like, so long as you stick to it, step by step.

Is it easy?
Make your steps small and easy and you'll be more likely to do them.

Are you ready to unblock it?
Have you thought about what could go wrong and how to deal with it?

FIVE TICKS? ✓✓✓✓✓
THEN GO FOR IT!

And that's how you do almost anything. This Easy 4-Step Plan really works, whatever you want to do, so long as you follow it carefully, making all the steps really small and easy for yourself.

Still a bit doubtful?

THAT'S EASY FOR YOU TO SAY!

Don't worry, you can do it.

The E4SP really works, even when you have a really tough problem to deal with.

Remember the elephant – you can eat it piece by piece. All you have to do is keep on eating!

And don't beat yourself up if things go wrong half way through. Just calmly go back to the plan and take those small, steady steps again.

But what about when your enthusiasm goes? When the novelty wears off and you can't remember why you went to all this trouble in the first place?

That's when you need the next two pages!

WHAT TO DO WHEN THE GOING GETS TOUGH

Remind yourself why you're doing this

If you're having trouble keeping going, say, in the middle of your plan when things are getting difficult, try these ideas to remind yourself why you started in the first place.

- Write down the reasons you want to do this and put them where you can see them.
- Think about the state you'll be in in 2 or 3 years time if you give in now. Write that down and stick it where you can see it.
- Think about the advantages of succeeding – better health, better relationships, keeping a job down, having more friends, having more fun, having more money, doing better overall. Write those down and put them where you can see them.
- Tell as many people as possible what you're doing, so that they can help you (or remind you when you slip).

Ready for some real-life examples?

If you're not sure how to apply the E4SP to your problem. the next few pages will help.

They're full of real plans, showing how people like you have fixed different things and turned their lives around.

How the **E4SP** works in real life

I WANT TO MAKE NEW FRIENDS

Step 1.

How do you break 'making new friends' into little chunks? Change it to 'make *one* new friend'. It's a lot easier to work at finding and connecting with one person than to try to transform yourself into the life and soul of the neighbourhood.

So let's say your chosen chunk is 'Find and make one new friend'. You can always repeat the process when you've succeeded.

Step 2.

Here's how your brainstorm might go:
- List and look up old friends that you've lost touch with.
- List the people you know already that you'd like to be a friend.
- Stop eating alone in the canteen and sit with other people.
- Join a networking website like Facebook or Friends Reunited.
- Ask people you know to introduce you to other people.
- Ask classmates or workmates if they have sisters or brothers that you could meet.
- Join a club or society. If it involves sport or fitness, you could crack two problems at once! (See 'Get fitter' and 'Lose weight').

Step 3.

Let's choose idea 1 and make a plan.
- Look up the phone numbers, email and street addresses of old friends.

- Write a letter or email to those whose phone number you don't know. Now take the list of old friends with phones and choose just one.
- Call them up.
- Repeat this process with the next person on your list.

Step 4.

Check the plan (see pages 10 & 11) and if you have 5 ticks, go for it.

Get out your old phone book, scroll through those old numbers or click on your email address book and make a list of the people you're going to contact.

Write that letter or email, making it chatty, full of questions about them and news about yourself. Invite a reply with their news.

Now do the call. Say you've been thinking about your old friend and wondered how he or she was doing. Continue the conversation by asking lots of questions. Keep the focus on your friend and use questioning words like *who, what, why, when* and *how*.

In your conversation, look for common ground and shared interests.

Finish the chat with an invitation to have another talk, or a coffee together somewhere. If your old friend agrees, make a firm arrangement there and then.

And remember, if this plan doesn't work out, or it gets too much for you in the middle, don't beat yourself up, just go back to the brainstorm and pick another idea to try!

Good Luck!

I WANT TO GET A JOB

Step 1.
Another huge, elephant-like objective.
So let's break it into little chunks.

Chunk: work out what you want to do

Chunk: learn the skills you need to get a job you'll like

Chunk: find out what jobs are available

Chunk: get an interview

Step 2.
Let's brainstorm that first chunk – working out what you want to do. You could:
- Go to the library and get some books about finding the right career.
- Think about the things you enjoy doing and are good at.
- Make a list of your knowledge.
- Make a list of what you value as an activity or career.
- Ask friends and family what they think you're good at.
- Go to a careers adviser at school or your university or at the jobcentre and talk to them

Steps 3 and 4.

This is a situation in which the brainstorm almost wrote the plan. You could put those ideas into practice, one by one, and you'd be very likely to end up knowing what kind of job you'd enjoy and could probably do.

Then you could move on to chunk 2 and brainstorm/plan how to get any additional skills you might need.

Work your way steadily through the chunks, using the E4SP each time and you'll be giving yourself the best possible chance to get a job.

Meantime, remember this: as soon as you start on this plan, you have a job! You are fully employed using the E4SP to find work.

Good Luck!

I WANT TO LOSE WEIGHT

Step 1.
First point: don't eat an elephant – they're fattening.

Second point: losing weight is easy to break into little pieces. Don't say 'I'm going to lose 12 kilos' say 'I'm going to lose 1 kilo'.

So step 1 in the E4SP for weight loss is: choose a SMALL chunk of weight to lose. Let's say 1 kilo.

Step 2.
The brainstorm, could include:
- Join a weight-loss group.
- Walk to a friends or work each day or get off the bus a stop earlier.
- Go walking or running with friends.
- Don't use lifts or escalators.
- Cut out chocolate, ice cream, buns, cheese or puddings (have fruit instead).
- Tell your friends about your target so they help you keep to it.
- Eat nothing but broccoli for a month (OK, this is a whacky one and would probably damage your social life, but this is a brainstorm, remember?).
- Write down all the reasons you can think of for losing weight (health, fitness, attractiveness to others, etc) and stick them on the fridge.
- Write down all the bad things about excess weight you can think of and stick them on the fridge as well (heart disease, cancer, blood pressure, strokes, diabetes).

Now let's say you chose brainstorm idea 1 – the weight loss group. (Incidentally, weight loss is one of the problems where doing more than one idea at once is good, so those notices on the fridge are a great idea whatever main plan you're following.)

Step 3.
Step 3, the plan, could include:
- Get online and find the local Weightwatchers (or similar) branch.
- Get the phone number and call them.
- Talk to a friend who also wants to lose weight and see if they want to go with you.
- Arrange to go to just one meeting to see what it's like.
- Go to one meeting next Monday (getting off the bus early or walking there if possible).
- Join up if you like the idea.
- Follow the recommended plan.
- Lose weight!

Step 4.
Does your plan score 5 ticks (see pages 10 & 11)? If so, get online (or look in the local Yellow Pages) and make a start.

And remember, if it doesn't work for you – weight loss groups aren't everyone's thing – all you have to do is go back to the brainstorm, pick another idea and make a plan for that.

Good Luck!

I WANT TO STOP OVERSPENDING

Some of the chunks that you could break this problem into involve understanding why and when you do it.

Working on an understanding of the problem before actually trying to fix it is perfectly OK. The better you understand yourself, the more chance you have of getting in control of what you do. Chunks could be:

- Work out when I overspend (By myself? With friends? When I have new money?).
- Work out why I overspend. (When I'm upset? Lonely? Angry? When I need a boost?).
- Work out if it's it like an addiction. Do I think about what I'm going to get all the time?
- Am I trying to prove myself to someone else?
- Am I doing this for the excitement?
- Don't stop spending altogether, but decide not to make impulse buys.
- Don't stop spending altogether, but decide not to shop online.

Let's say you choose no 6 – no more impulse buys. So that's **Step 1.**

Step 2.

Your brainstorm ideas could include:

- Always use shopping lists.
- Impose a 24 hour 'cooling off' period when you see something you fancy.
- Take your credit cards out of your purse and keep them in a drawer at home.

- Cut up all but one of your credit cards – the one that's spent up.
- Decide to only use cash when shopping.
- Don't go shopping unless there is something specific you need.
- Don't go shopping alone – take a sensible friend or relative with you.

Step 3.

OK. Let's say you decide on idea 5 – cash only. Now you need to make a plan. It might look like this

Go to the cash point and get out only enough money for today's bus fares and lunch.

Go home and put your cashpoint card in a drawer.

When you go out, if you see a CD you want, you can't buy it today, but you could plan to buy it tomorrow.

Tonight, get out enough cash for tomorrow's bus fares, lunch and the CD.

Tomorrow, leave cashpoint card at home but buy CD with cash.

In the evening, get out only enough cash for tomorrow's bus fares and lunch.

Step 4.

Check your plan for the five ticks (pages 10 & 11) and if it passes the test, put it into action!

And don't worry. If you slip, or find you can't control your spending this way, go back to the chunks and pick another one to work on.

Good Luck!

I NEED TO REVISE FOR EXAMS

Step 1.
Almost everyone is worried about exams and sometimes you can get like a rabbit in the headlights – there's so much to do, so many subjects to revise that you just can't get started.

This is where the chunking idea is really handy – and really obvious. Don't try and revise everything, just do one subject at a time. So your chunks could be: History • Geography • English • Maths • Science … and so on. What chunk to choose? Let's say History – So that's **Step 1.**

Step 2.
A brainstorm about ways to revise History could come up with ideas like these:

- Write out the History syllabus and read the chapters one by one.
- Make a timetable so that you cover everything by the exam.
- Find a friend who's doing the same exam and work together.
- Divide your week into revision periods and don't go out or watch TV at those times.
- Decide on three days a week for revision and text your friends to say your phone will be off on those days.
- Pitch a tent in the garden and do all your revision in there, away from the TV.
- Go to the library and get some books out about revision technique.
- Go and stay with your granny who only has a black & white TV.

Step 3.
Let's say you choose idea 3 – find a friend and work together.

This is what your plan could include.

Call your friends in the same class, one by one, and outline your idea.

Do a deal with the first one who agrees.

Get together and decide on a day to start work

Decide on a place to work

Discuss the revision methods you will use – testing each other?

Revising out loud?

Have a plan for when motivation fades.

Discuss and agree a system of small rewards for good work. Maybe the cinema once a week.

Step 4.

Check your plan for 5 ticks (pages 10 & 11) and put it into action. And remember, you'll need motivation, especially when you've done the first couple of subjects and you're switching to maths, or something you don't like.

Here are some of the things you could stick on the wall of your revision room to remind you why you're doing this:
- Better exam results mean a better career and more money.
- Bad exam results mean little choice of what you do in life.
- Bad exam results only mean you'll have to do it all again next year.
- Most people flunk exams through not working.
- You'll feel great when you've done each subject and can reward yourself.
- A good performance in exams usually means a great summer holiday.

Good Luck!

NOW IT'S YOUR TURN!

As the real life examples show, the E4SP works really well. All you have to do is take it step by step and be steady and determined. If one of the ready-made plans you've just seen fits the bill, please use it!
If you need to make one for yourself, get that piece of paper now and start breaking your elephant into bits!

Good Luck!

ABOUT THIS BOOK

With websites receiving over 4 million hits a month and a wealth of supporting research data, the Five Areas Approach on which this book is based, devised by Dr Chris Williams, is one of the most widely-used CBT systems in the world.

Cognitive Behavioural Therapy (CBT) has a strong evidence base for helping people with low mood, anxiety and a growing range of other common mental and physical health difficulties.

Want to learn more about you? Turn things around in your life for the better? The Five Areas Approach can help you to do this. It takes the proven CBT model and makes it accessible and practical so that you can have the tools you need to help change things in your life – fast.

Please visit the Five Areas websites – www.llttf.com (free life skills course), www.llttfshop.com (bookshop) and www.fiveareasonline.com (online books) – to discover more about this work and see the other resources on offer.

Dr Chris Williams is Professor of Psychosocial Psychiatry at the University of Glasgow, UK, and is a past-President of the British Association for Behavioural and Cognitive Psychotherapies (www.babcp.com) – the lead body for CBT in the UK, Patron of the charities Anxiety UK and Triumph over Phobia and is a well-known CBT workshop leader and researcher.

PICK ME UP

Turn your life around – fast!

Available in the Pick Me Up range:

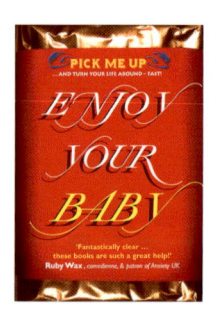

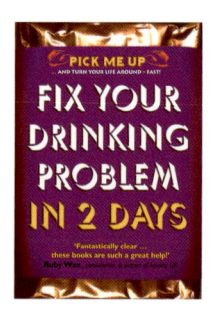

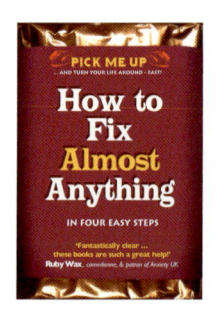

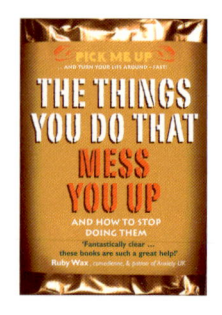

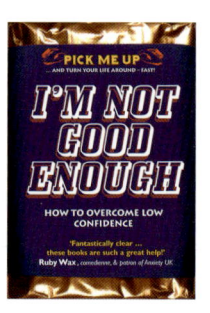

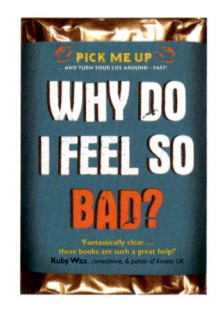

- **Enjoy Your Baby**
- **Fix Your Drinking Problem in 2 Days**
- **How to Fix Almost Anything** — In Four Easy Steps
- **The Things You Do That Mess You Up** — And How to Stop Doing Them
- **I'm Not Good Enough** — How to Overcome Low Confidence
- **Why Do I Feel So Bad?**